2016 SQA Past Papers With Answers

National 5
GERMAN

FREE
audio files to accompany this title can be
accessed at
www.hoddergibson.co.uk
• Click on the turquoise 'Updates and Extras' box.
• Look for the 'SQA Papers Audio Files' heading
and click the 'Browse' button beneath.
• You will then find the files listed
by language and level.

2014, 2015 & 2016 Exams

Hodder Gibson Study Skills Advice – General	– page 3
Hodder Gibson Study Skills Advice – National 5 German	– page 5
2014 EXAM	– page 9
2015 EXAM	– page 39
2016 EXAM	– page 69
ANSWERS	– page 99

(side spine text) National 5 GERMAN

HODDER
GIBSON
AN HACHETTE UK COMPANY

This book contains the official SQA 2014, 2015 and 2016 Exams for National 5 German, with associated SQA-approved answers modified from the official marking instructions that accompany the paper.

In addition the book contains study skills advice. This advice has been specially commissioned by Hodder Gibson, and has been written by experienced senior teachers and examiners in line with the new National 5 syllabus and assessment outlines. This is not SQA material but has been devised to provide further guidance for National 5 examinations.

Hodder Gibson is grateful to the copyright holders, as credited on the final page of the Answer Section, for permission to use their material. Every effort has been made to trace the copyright holders and to obtain their permission for the use of copyright material. Hodder Gibson will be happy to receive information allowing us to rectify any error or omission in future editions.

Hachette UK's policy is to use papers that are natural, renewable and recyclable products and made from wood grown in sustainable forests. The logging and manufacturing processes are expected to conform to the environmental regulations of the country of origin.

Orders: please contact Bookpoint Ltd, 130 Park Drive, Milton Park, Abingdon, Oxon OX14 4SE. Telephone: (44) 01235 827720. Fax: (44) 01235 400454. Lines are open 9.00–5.00, Monday to Saturday, with a 24-hour message answering service. Visit our website at www.hoddereducation.co.uk. Hodder Gibson can be contacted direct on: Tel: 0141 333 4650; Fax: 0141 404 8188; email: hoddergibson@hodder.co.uk

This collection first published in 2016 by
Hodder Gibson, an imprint of Hodder Education,
An Hachette UK Company
211 St Vincent Street
Glasgow G2 5QY

Typeset by Aptara, Inc.

Printed in the UK

A catalogue record for this title is available from the British Library

ISBN: 978-1-4718-9111-3

3 2 1

2017 2016

Introduction
Study Skills – what you need to know to pass exams!

Pause for thought

Many students might skip quickly through a page like this. After all, we all know how to revise. Do you really though?

Think about this:

"IF YOU ALWAYS DO WHAT YOU ALWAYS DO, YOU WILL ALWAYS GET WHAT YOU HAVE ALWAYS GOT."

Do you like the grades you get? Do you want to do better? If you get full marks in your assessment, then that's great! Change nothing! This section is just to help you get that little bit better than you already are.

There are two main parts to the advice on offer here. The first part highlights fairly obvious things but which are also very important. The second part makes suggestions about revision that you might not have thought about but which WILL help you.

Part 1

DOH! It's so obvious but …

Start revising in good time

Don't leave it until the last minute – this will make you panic.

Make a revision timetable that sets out work time AND play time.

Sleep and eat!

Obvious really, and very helpful. Avoid arguments or stressful things too – even games that wind you up. You need to be fit, awake and focused!

Know your place!

Make sure you know exactly **WHEN and WHERE** your exams are.

Know your enemy!

Make sure you know what to expect in the exam.

How is the paper structured?

How much time is there for each question?

What types of question are involved?

Which topics seem to come up time and time again?

Which topics are your strongest and which are your weakest?

Are all topics compulsory or are there choices?

Learn by DOING!

There is no substitute for past papers and practice papers – they are simply essential! Tackling this collection of papers and answers is exactly the right thing to be doing as your exams approach.

Part 2

People learn in different ways. Some like low light, some bright. Some like early morning, some like evening / night. Some prefer warm, some prefer cold. But everyone uses their BRAIN and the brain works when it is active. Passive learning – sitting gazing at notes – is the most INEFFICIENT way to learn anything. Below you will find tips and ideas for making your revision more effective and maybe even more enjoyable. What follows gets your brain active, and active learning works!

Activity 1 – Stop and review

Step 1

When you have done no more than 5 minutes of revision reading STOP!

Step 2

Write a heading in your own words which sums up the topic you have been revising.

Step 3

Write a summary of what you have revised in no more than two sentences. Don't fool yourself by saying, "I know it, but I cannot put it into words". That just means you don't know it well enough. If you cannot write your summary, revise that section again, knowing that you must write a summary at the end of it. Many of you will have notebooks full of blue/black ink writing. Many of the pages will not be especially attractive or memorable so try to liven them up a bit with colour as you are reviewing and rewriting. **This is a great memory aid, and memory is the most important thing.**

Activity 2 – Use technology!

Why should everything be written down? Have you thought about "mental" maps, diagrams, cartoons and colour to help you learn? And rather than write down notes, why not record your revision material?

What about having a text message revision session with friends? Keep in touch with them to find out how and what they are revising and share ideas and questions.

Why not make a video diary where you tell the camera what you are doing, what you think you have learned and what you still have to do? No one has to see or hear it, but the process of having to organise your thoughts in a formal way to explain something is a very important learning practice.

Be sure to make use of electronic files. You could begin to summarise your class notes. Your typing might be slow, but it will get faster and the typed notes will be easier to read than the scribbles in your class notes. Try to add different fonts and colours to make your work stand out. You can easily Google relevant pictures, cartoons and diagrams which you can copy and paste to make your work more attractive and **MEMORABLE**.

Activity 3 – This is it. Do this and you will know lots!

Step 1

In this task you must be very honest with yourself! Find the SQA syllabus for your subject (www.sqa.org.uk). Look at how it is broken down into main topics called MANDATORY knowledge. That means stuff you MUST know.

Step 2

BEFORE you do ANY revision on this topic, write a list of everything that you already know about the subject. It might be quite a long list but you only need to write it once. It shows you all the information that is already in your long-term memory so you know what parts you do not need to revise!

Step 3

Pick a chapter or section from your book or revision notes. Choose a fairly large section or a whole chapter to get the most out of this activity.

With a buddy, use Skype, Facetime, Twitter or any other communication you have, to play the game "If this is the answer, what is the question?". For example, if you are revising Geography and the answer you provide is "meander", your buddy would have to make up a question like "What is the word that describes a feature of a river where it flows slowly and bends often from side to side?".

Make up 10 "answers" based on the content of the chapter or section you are using. Give this to your buddy to solve while you solve theirs.

Step 4

Construct a wordsearch of at least 10 × 10 squares. You can make it as big as you like but keep it realistic. Work together with a group of friends. Many apps allow you to make wordsearch puzzles online. The words and phrases can go in any direction and phrases can be split. Your puzzle must only contain facts linked to the topic you are revising. Your task is to find 10 bits of information to hide in your puzzle, but you must not repeat information that you used in Step 3. DO NOT show where the words are. Fill up empty squares with random letters. Remember to keep a note of where your answers are hidden but do not show your friends. When you have a complete puzzle, exchange it with a friend to solve each other's puzzle.

Step 5

Now make up 10 questions (not "answers" this time) based on the same chapter used in the previous two tasks. Again, you must find NEW information that you have not yet used. Now it's getting hard to find that new information! Again, give your questions to a friend to answer.

Step 6

As you have been doing the puzzles, your brain has been actively searching for new information. Now write a NEW LIST that contains only the new information you have discovered when doing the puzzles. Your new list is the one to look at repeatedly for short bursts over the next few days. Try to remember more and more of it without looking at it. After a few days, you should be able to add words from your second list to your first list as you increase the information in your long-term memory.

FINALLY! Be inspired...

Make a list of different revision ideas and beside each one write **THINGS I HAVE** tried, **THINGS I WILL** try and **THINGS I MIGHT** try. Don't be scared of trying something new.

And remember – "FAIL TO PREPARE AND PREPARE TO FAIL!"

National 5 German

You have chosen to add a national qualification in German to your education. Congratulations – it is one of the most sought-after foreign languages for business and trade in Scotland and in Europe.

What can National 5 do for you?

National 5 German is a course which has been developed by teachers and educational leaders to meet the requirements for Modern Foreign Languages in the 21st century.

The aim of the course is to give you confidence in understanding (reading and listening) and using (speaking and writing) German in the following contexts:

- Society (Family and friends, Lifestyle, Media, Global languages, Citizenship)
- Learning (Learning in context, Education)
- Employability (Jobs, Work and CVs)
- Culture (Planning a trip, Other countries, Celebrating a special event, German literature, German films and TV)

What does the Course Assessment look like?

Reading and Writing

You will have 1 hour and 30 minutes for both parts of this paper. This question paper will have 50 marks in total – 50% of the overall course marks.

The Reading paper

The reading part of this paper will have 30 marks – 10 marks for each text.

You will read three German texts of between 150 and 200 words each. Questions on the text are set in English, and you must respond in English. These questions will ask for specific details about the text, but there will also be an **overall purpose question**.

You may use a dictionary in this paper.

What is the "overall purpose"?

Whenever you read a text (or listen to a text) in any language, you should be aware that texts are produced for a reason and/or a certain audience. This could be to advertise a product, to promote a place of interest, to express concern about a situation, to invite somebody to an event, to give an opinion about a matter – to name but a few. This should sound familiar to you from your English classes.

You will have to show understanding of the overall purpose of a text in your course assessment in Reading and in Listening by answering a supported question (multiple choice) correctly.

The Writing paper

You will produce one written text, a job application in German, in response to a stimulus supported by six bullet points which you must address. See them as a checklist of information that you will have to provide in your response.

Four of the bullet points are predictable but two of them are less predictable as they vary from year to year.

The text you produce must take the form of an e-mail and should be between 120 to 150 words in length.

You may use a dictionary in this paper.

Listening

The Listening paper

This question paper will have 20 marks – 20% of the total mark.

You will listen to one monologue (approximately one and a half minutes long) and one short dialogue (approximately two to two and a half minutes long) in German. You will be asked questions in English and must respond in English.

The monologue is worth 8 marks and it is necessary for you to understand the overall purpose of the spoken text (see *What is the "overall purpose"?*, below left).

The dialogue is worth 12 marks and it has a topical link to the monologue.

You may not use a dictionary in this paper.

Speaking

The speaking assessment will be carried out in your school by your German teacher, who will be able to help you to prepare for it well in advance. It will be recorded and marked by your teacher.

The speaking assessment has two parts:

1 A presentation in German on a topic of your choice, such as:

- Meine Familie und ich
- Meine Freizeit und meine Freunde
- Meine Heimatstadt
- Meine Schule und meine Schulkarriere
- Meine Zukunftspläne
- Mein Arbeitspraktikum
- Mein Lieblingsfilm
- Mein Lieblingsbuch

The presentation should be approximately two to three minutes long, you may use notes (not sentences) and/or visual support such as a PowerPoint presentation, a picture, a photograph, an item, etc.

2 A discussion with your teacher in German

Your teacher will ask you additional questions on your presentation or may ask questions which relate to a topic derived from your presentation. The discussion should be approximately three to five minutes long.

The total mark for your speaking exam at National 5 is 30. Five out of these 30 marks will only be granted if the language you use in the conversation is natural and spontaneous.

What can you do to help you have a successful National 5 German exam?

Top Tip: Do not panic!

As soon as the exam timetable is published, ask your teacher for the exact date of the German exam (usually April/May time) and mark the date and time in your diary – or on your mobile phone.

Remember that your Speaking exam will be done before your Reading and Writing and Listening exams. Take this into account when you plan your revision.

Reading tips

Before you read the German texts:

- read the title/headline and ask yourself what you already know about the topic.
- look at any pictures as they support the contents of a text.
- check if the text comes with a glossary to save yourself time looking up words in the dictionary.

While you are reading the German texts:

- focus on your reading – be an active reader!
- try to figure out the main idea(s) of the text(s).
- access the meaning of a word by
  - checking the context/sentence the word is in.
  - checking if the word is similar to English (German and English have many cognates or near cognates – which are words that look and/ or sound similar or even the same); many German and English words begin with the same letter or even the same two letters.
  - checking whether or not the text comes with a glossary.
  - using the dictionary.

After you have read the text and before you start answering the questions:

- read the comprehension questions carefully.
- if necessary, underline the question word to highlight exactly what kind of answer is required.
- check the tense form of the English question to make sure you use the same tense form in your answer.
- make sure that your answer has sufficient detail – compare it with the marks you can get for each answer.

Most importantly – make sure your English answers make sense and your English expression is of a good standard.

After you have answered the questions:

- allow yourself time to go over your answers.

Writing tips

Before you sit your writing exam:

- plan the exam carefully by exploring the four predictable bullet points:
  - Make sure you know the proper conventions for your piece of writing and practise them.
  - Make a note of some vocabulary which you will need to address these bullet points and learn it. Choose five verbs, five adjectives and five nouns, for example.
  - Remember what you have practised in class when covering the topic areas you are writing about.
  - Produce a draft and show it to your teacher before the exam.

While you are sitting your writing exam:

- read the stimulus very carefully and identify exactly what the job is that you are going to apply for. Use the dictionary for help, if necessary, and remember that jobs in German have male and female forms.
- read the two bullet points which are less predictable. Remember what you have learned in class about the topics they address.
- avoid writing very long sentences as you may lose control of structure and word order. However, try to include connectors such as und/aber/oder/denn and also some which change the word order such as weil/obwohl/dass.
- try to use different tense forms where possible, e.g. "Ich habe im letzten Jahr ein Arbeitspraktikum gemacht."/ "Ich werde das Abitur machen und Deutsch studieren."

- where possible, include opinions using German expressions such as "Ich denke, dass..."/ "Ich bin der Meinung, dass..."/"Ich finde..."/"Meiner Meinung nach..."
- try not to translate from English as you will be tempted to apply the English sentence structure rather than the German one – focus on the correct position of the verb in the German sentence and remember the rules of German sentence structure.
- limit yourself to 20 to 25 words per bullet point and make sure you address them all.
- focus on capitalisation of nouns and correct verb endings to achieve a high level of accuracy.

After you have finished your writing exam:

- leave yourself enough time at the end to proofread your e-mail text.
- check that you have addressed all six bullet points.
- check your verb endings and tense forms, your adjective endings and capitalisation of nouns.
- if in doubt, use the dictionary for support.

Listening tips

Top Tip: Learn your vocabulary regularly and revise systematically before the exam. Only those who recognise words will be able to understand the meaning of a spoken sentence.

Before you sit your listening exam:

- revise vocabulary, especially verbs in their different tense forms, quantifiers (viel, wenig, die meisten), numbers and dates. Read vocabulary out loud so that you recognise acoustically what you see in front of you.
- read the title/the introduction to the listening item and ask yourself what your experience with the topic is and what you know about this topic.
- remember the close relationship between the English and the German language where many words sound very similar and use this to your benefit in listening. However, beware: "Schinken" is not "chicken"!
- read the English questions very carefully – you have one minute to study them – and underline the question words or any others which you feel might be of importance.
- remember that the questions are in chronological sequence – the answer to question (c) must be between the answers to (b) and (d) in the recording.

While you are sitting your listening exam:

- remember that both items (monologue and dialogue) will be played three times so it is not necessary to answer any questions during the first playing.
- write your answers neatly and clearly on your question paper. If you correct your answer, make sure the marker will be able to recognise your final answer.
- if you don't understand a word which you believe to be an element of an answer – do not panic! Trust your instincts and your natural connection to German as a speaker of English and see if you can guess the meaning.
- be guided by the number of marks allocated to each question. They will tell you how much information is expected in your answer.

After your listening exam:

- go over your answers. Make sure your English expression is as good as possible to convey meaning clearly.
- make sure you have crossed out any draft answers leaving the final answer for the marker to see.

Speaking tips

Top tips:

- **Start preparing for your speaking exam in plenty of time. Practise speaking regularly as practice makes perfect.**
- **Remember that your teacher will conduct the exam and that he/she will want to help you to succeed. Trust him/her.**

Before your speaking exam:

- choose a topic that you really like and have something to say about for your presentation.
- develop a piece of writing for your presentation which has a clear structure. Show this work to your teacher.
- ask your teacher to read aloud and record this text for you on your mobile phone, iPod or any other media device so that you can listen to it many times before the exam.
- turn the sentences of that text into notes. (A note is a short phrase which does not contain a verb.)
- practise your presentation by listening to the recording and reading your notes, then try it without the recording by your teacher.
- try to figure out what kind of questions your teacher might ask you in the discussion. These questions will be linked to the topic you have presented.

For example:

If you have done a presentation on your favourite film, your teacher might ask questions such as:

- "Siehst du gern fern oder gehst du lieber ins Kino?"
- "Was findest du besser – DVDs zu Hause oder einen Kinofilm mit Freunden?"
- "Hast du einen Lieblingsschauspieler/eine Lieblings-schauspielerin? Warum findest du ihn/sie gut?"
- "Welche Filme siehst du gern?"
- "Welche Fernsehsendungen siehst du gern?"

Make sure you revise and learn conventions on expressing an opinion in German, e.g. "Ich finde ...", "Ich bin der Meinung, dass...", "Meiner Meinung nach..." etc.

You should also revise and learn conventions on how to sustain a conversation – especially when you have difficulties understanding a question, e.g. "Ich habe das nicht verstanden. Bitte wiederholen Sie die Frage."/ "Ich bin nicht sicher, was das auf Deutsch/Englisch heißt."/ "Sprechen Sie bitte langsamer."

During your speaking exam:

- concentrate on your notes in your presentation. You are entitled to use them – do not do without.
- look up from your notes, keep eye contact and speak loudly and clearly to show you are confident – and to ensure a good quality of recording!
- do not panic if you are stuck – try to recover by remembering what you have worked out for your presentation.
- listen carefully to your teacher's questions and remember that you can always "steal" vocabulary from the question to make your answer.
- try to avoid very long sentences as you might lose control over the sentence structure. However, try to use connectors such as und/aber/oder/denn and also weil.
- ask for help (in German) when you need it. This will not necessarily result in a lower mark as it shows your ability to use German for clarification purposes.

After your speaking exam:

- ask your teacher if it is possible to listen to your recording and get some feedback on your performance.
- you might want to use your National 5 speaking exam as a basis for your Higher speaking exam – so keep your notes if you are thinking about taking Higher German.

In your National 5 Course Assessment, the formula to success is a sound knowledge of the level of German required, teamwork in class and with your teacher, and confidence in yourself and the skills your teacher has helped you to develop. Most importantly though, enjoy the course and the experience. Deutsch ist mega cool!

Good luck!

Remember that the rewards for passing National 5 German are well worth it! Your pass will help you get the future you want for yourself. In the exam, be confident in your own ability. If you're not sure how to answer a question, trust your instincts and just give it a go anyway. Keep calm and don't panic! GOOD LUCK!

NATIONAL 5

2014

N5

National
Qualifications
2014

Mark

X734/75/01

**German
Reading**

TUESDAY, 20 MAY

9:00 AM – 10:30 AM

Fill in these boxes and read what is printed below.

Full name of centre

Town

Forename(s)

Surname

Number of seat

Date of birth

Day	Month	Year

Scottish candidate number

Total marks — 30

Attempt ALL questions.

Write your answers clearly, in **English**, in the spaces provided in this booklet.

You may use a German dictionary.

Additional space for answers is provided at the end of this booklet. If you use this space you must clearly identify the question number you are attempting.

Use **blue** or **black** ink.

There is a separate question and answer booklet for Writing. You must complete your answer for Writing in the question and answer booklet for Writing.

Before leaving the examination room you must give both booklets to the Invigilator; if you do not, you may lose all the marks for this paper.

Total marks — 30

Attempt ALL questions

Text 1

You read a magazine article about COOL-Centers, a recent development in German schools.

Im dritten Stock meiner Schule ist das COOL-Center. COOL heißt COoperatives Offenes Lernen, ein System, wo Schüler mit einem Lehrer in einer kleinen Gruppe arbeiten — es ist für die Schüler die Chance, ihre Arbeit mit anderen Schülern und Lehrern zu diskutieren und ihre Talente und Ideen zu entwickeln.

Das COOL-System hat viele Vorteile — in kleinen Gruppen kann man alles besser planen. Man hat viel Freiheit und man lernt, unabhängig zu sein.

Die siebzehnjährige Inge Schönefeld geht jeden Tag sehr gern ins COOL-Center: „Ich war schon immer ein bisschen schüchtern und in einer normalen Schulklasse habe ich nie etwas gesagt. Im COOL-Center dagegen habe ich alle Schüler in meiner Gruppe kennen gelernt und ich habe keine Angst, meine Meinung zu sagen."

„Auch für den späteren Beruf ist das COOL-Center etwas Positives: in der Gruppe lernt man, wie man sich am besten auf ein Interview vorbereitet. Ich habe zum Beispiel gelernt, dass das Aussehen immer sehr wichtig ist. Ich kann jetzt besser Augenkontakt halten, was für mich früher unmöglich war und vor allem habe ich gelernt, langsamer und deutlicher zu sprechen."

Questions

(a) What does the COOL-Center give pupils the chance to do? Mention **two** things.

    2

_____

_____

(b) What are the advantages of this system of learning? Mention any **two** things.

    2

_____

_____

MARKS | DO NOT WRITE IN THIS MARGIN

Text 1 Questions (continued)

(c) (i) What kind of person was Inge before she attended the COOL-Center? Mention **one** thing.

1

_____

(ii) In what way has Inge benefitted from being at the COOL-Center? Mention **two** things.

2

_____

_____

(d) The COOL-Center has helped Inge prepare for job interviews.

What has she learnt? Mention any **two** things.

2

_____

_____

(e) Reading the passage as a whole, who do you think the COOL-Center is intended for?

Tick (✓) the correct box.

1

Pupils with learning difficulties.	
Pupils who prefer to work independently.	
Pupils who like working with others.	

[Turn over

Text 2

You read an article about the future of the cinema in Germany.

'Immer weniger Menschen gehen ins Kino' — *'Angst um die Zukunft der deutschen Filmindustrie'*.

Jens Pfarnauer ist Direktor eines kleinen Stadtkinos in Leipzig, und er weiß, dass es momentan ernste Probleme gibt: „Im vergangenen Jahr sind etwa 30% weniger Menschen durch die Tür gekommen. Woran liegt das? Die (inter)nationale Wirtschaftskrise spielt eine Rolle — viele Menschen haben einfach weniger Geld zur Verfügung."

Im großen Kinocenter am Stadtrand sieht es aber anders aus. „Bei uns läuft das Geschäft gut", so Karli Hägerich vom Odeonkino. „Wir haben genug Parkplätze für alle; an zwei Tagen in der Woche haben wir Karten im Sonderangebot und wir haben 10% Ermäßigung für regelmäßige Kinobesucher."

Es gibt natürlich viele Gründe, nicht mehr ins Kino zu gehen. Immer mehr Menschen haben große Bildschirme zu Hause. Man kann auf Pause drücken, wenn man will und man kann die neusten Kinohits direkt aus dem Internet herunterladen.

3D-Produktionen aber können eine bessere Zukunft für deutsche Kinos schaffen. Im letzten Jahr sind sieben deutsche 3D-Filme im Kino erschienen; das sind mehr als in jedem anderen Land – mit Ausnahme der USA!

Questions

(a) What statistic does Jens Pfarnauer quote to prove that the German film industry is in trouble? Complete the sentence.

1

Last year saw a 30% drop in _____.

(b) What reason is given for the film industry being in trouble? Mention any **one** thing.

1

_____

(c) Karli Hägerich has seen her cinema do well recently. What things have they done to attract business? Mention **three** things.

3

_____

_____

_____

MARKS

DO NOT WRITE IN THIS MARGIN

Text 2 Questions (continued)

(d) What reasons are there for staying in and watching movies at home? Mention **three** things.

3

_____

_____

_____

(e) Cinemas are hoping that 3D movies will help them survive. What shows that these films are doing well in Germany? Mention **two** things.

2

_____

_____

[Turn over

Text 3

As part of a whole school project on Africa you have been asked to read this article in the German class.

Ohne Wasser gibt es kein Leben!

Das Wasser ist sehr wichtig für das Leben von Pflanzen, Tieren und Menschen. Wir brauchen es zum Kleiderwaschen, Kochen, Abspülen und Duschen.

In den meisten europäischen Ländern führt zu jedem Haus eine Leitung mit sauberem Wasser. Aber viele Menschen in Afrika haben kein Wasser in ihren Häusern. Sie holen sich das Wasser von einem Brunnen im Dorf oder sie müssen zum Fluss gehen. Oft ist das Wasser verschmutzt. Das ist sehr gefährlich, besonders für Kinder. Schmutziges Trinkwasser führt zu schweren Krankheiten und ist leider oft tödlich.

Aber auch in Deutschland gibt es Probleme mit verschmutztem Wasser. Viele deutsche Fabriken benutzen eine Menge chemische Produkte. Diese Produkte sind manchmal giftig und fließen in die Flüsse. Dann sterben Tausende von Fischen und Vögeln.

In Europa benutzen die Menschen zu viel Wasser. Ein Deutscher verbraucht täglich ungefähr 120 Liter Wasser, das sind zwölf Eimer voll mit Wasser. Wir sollten Wasser sparen, zum Beispiel: die Pflanzen im Garten nicht mehr als einmal die Woche giessen, den Wasserhahn nicht laufen lassen und die Spülmaschine nur anschalten, wenn sie voll ist.

Questions

(a) According to the article, what do people use water for?

Tick (✓) the **two** correct statements.

2

Washing the kitchen	
Washing clothes	
Showering	
Having a bath	

(b) In Africa lots of people have no water in their houses. Where do they fetch water from? Mention **two** things.

2

_____

_____

MARKS | DO NOT WRITE IN THIS MARGIN

Text 3 Questions (continued)

(c) Why is drinking dirty water dangerous for children? Mention **two** things.

2

_____

_____

(d) Why are German rivers polluted? Mention **two** things.

2

_____

_____

(e) Give any **two** examples of how we can save water.

2

_____

_____

[END OF QUESTION PAPER]

ADDITIONAL SPACE FOR ANSWERS

Page eight

MARKS | DO NOT WRITE IN THIS MARGIN

ADDITIONAL SPACE FOR ANSWERS

[BLANK PAGE]

DO NOT WRITE ON THIS PAGE

N5

National Qualifications 2014

Mark ☐

X734/75/02

German Writing

TUESDAY, 20 MAY
9:00 AM – 10:30 AM

___

Fill in these boxes and read what is printed below.

Full name of centre

Town

Forename(s)

Surname

Number of seat

Date of birth
Day   Month   Year

Scottish candidate number

Total marks — 20

Write your answer clearly, in **German**, in the space provided in this booklet.

You may use a German dictionary.

Additional space for answers is provided at the end of this booklet.

Use **blue** or **black** ink.

There is a separate question and answer booklet for Reading. You must complete your answers for Reading in the question and answer booklet for Reading.

Before leaving the examination room you must give both booklets to the Invigilator; if you do not, you may lose all the marks for this paper.

Total marks — 20

You are preparing an application for the job advertised below and write an e-mail in **German** to the company.

Bürohilfe — Office Services

Otto-Brenner-Straße,
30159 Hannover-Mitte

Unsere Firma in Hannover sucht zuverlässige, motivierte

Mitarbeiter/-innen in unserem Büro

mit guten Deutsch- und Englischkenntnissen. Sie sollten auch gut organisieren können.

Sie können uns unter info@buerohilfe-officeservices.de für weitere Information kontaktieren, oder uns Ihre Bewerbung schicken.

To help you to write your e-mail, you have been given the following checklist.

You must include **all** of these points:

- Personal details (name, age, where you live)
- School/college/education experience until now
- Skills/interests you have which make you right for the job
- Related work experience
- Any links you may have with a German-speaking country
- Any questions you may have about the job

Use all of the above to help you write the e-mail in **German**. The e-mail should be approximately 120 – 150 words. You may use a German dictionary.

ANSWER SPACE

MARKS

DO NOT
WRITE IN
THIS
MARGIN

[Turn over

MARKS | DO NOT WRITE IN THIS MARGIN

ANSWER SPACE (continued)

MARKS | DO NOT WRITE IN THIS MARGIN

ANSWER SPACE (continued)

[Turn over

MARKS DO NOT WRITE IN THIS MARGIN

ANSWER SPACE (continued)

[END OF QUESTION PAPER]

ADDITIONAL SPACE FOR ANSWERS

Page seven

ADDITIONAL SPACE FOR ANSWERS

N5

National
Qualifications
2014

Mark

X734/75/03

German
Listening

TUESDAY, 20 MAY

10:50 AM – 11:15 AM (approx)

Fill in these boxes and read what is printed below.

Full name of centre

Town

Forename(s)

Surname

Number of seat

Date of birth

Day	Month	Year
D D	M M	Y Y

Scottish candidate number

Total marks — 20

Attempt ALL questions.

Write your answers clearly, in **English**, in the spaces provided in this booklet. Additional space for answers is provided at the end of this booklet. If you use this space you must clearly identify the question number you are attempting.

Use **blue** or **black** ink.

You will hear two items in German. **Before you hear each item, you will have one minute to study the questions.** You will hear each item three times, with an interval of one minute between playings. You will then have time to answer the questions before hearing the next item.

You may take notes as you are listening to the German, but only in this booklet.

You may NOT use a German dictionary.

You are not allowed to leave the examination room until the end of the test.

Before leaving the examination room you must give this booklet to the Invigilator; if you do not, you may lose all the marks for this paper.

MARKS | DO NOT WRITE IN THIS MARGIN

Total marks — 20

Attempt ALL questions

Item 1

Annika, a sixteen year old German girl, is talking about her part-time job.

(a) How long has she had her part-time job? 1

_____

(b) What does her job at the supermarket involve? Mention any **one** thing. 1

_____

(c) Annika talks about her working hours. Complete the sentence. 1

Annika works on Saturdays between 08.00 and _____.

(d) (i) How much does Annika earn per hour? 1

_____

(ii) What does she think of this? 1

_____

(e) What does Annika say about her workmates? Mention any **one** thing. 1

_____

(f) What does she think of the work she has to do? Mention any **one** thing. 1

_____

(g) Think about what Annika has said.

What do you think are the reasons behind her choosing to talk about her part-time job?

Tick (✓) the correct statement. 1

Annika wants to tell the listener . . .

. . . about how she works part-time and also manages to help out at home.	
. . . her opinion of the work she does and of what she gets paid.	
. . . that a job brings financial independence from her parents.	

MARKS | DO NOT WRITE IN THIS MARGIN

Item 2

Annika continues in an interview.

(a) What year is Annika in?

1

_____

(b) What time does Annika have to get up in the morning?

1

_____

(c) What do Annika and her friend, Bensu, do in the afternoon after school? Mention any **one** thing.

1

_____

(d) What surprises the interviewer?

1

_____

(e) Annika says French is her best subject. What reasons does she give for this?

Tick (✓) the **two** correct statements.

2

She gets good marks.	
She is motivated in French.	
She simply finds foreign languages easy.	
She works as well as she can.	

(f) History was her worst subject at school. Give **two** reasons why this was the case.

2

_____

_____

(g) Annika is unsure about her long-term plans.

What does she say about her best friend, Lara? Mention **two** things.

2

_____

_____

MARKS | DO NOT WRITE IN THIS MARGIN

Item 2 (continued)

(h) Annika is thinking about going to university.

What might she do after she graduates from university? Mention **two** things.

2

_____

_____

[END OF QUESTION PAPER]

MARKS

ADDITIONAL SPACE FOR ANSWERS

Page five

MARKS DO NOT WRITE IN THIS MARGIN

ADDITIONAL SPACE FOR ANSWERS

Page six

National
Qualifications
2014

X734/75/13

German
Listening Transcript

TUESDAY, 20 MAY

10:50 AM – 11:15 AM (approx)

This paper must not be seen by any candidate.

The material overleaf is provided for use in an emergency only (eg the recording or equipment proving faulty) or where permission has been given in advance by SQA for the material to be read to candidates with additional support needs. The material must be read exactly as printed.

Instructions to reader(s):

For each item, read the English once, then read the German **three times**, with an interval of 1 minute between the three readings. On completion of the third reading, pause for the length of time indicated in brackets after the item, to allow the candidates to write their answers.

Where special arrangements have been agreed in advance to allow the reading of the material, those sections marked **(f)** should be read by a female speaker and those marked **(m)** by a male; those sections marked **(t)** should be read by the teacher.

(t)   Item number one.

Annika, a sixteen year old German girl, is talking about her part-time job.

You now have one minute to study the questions for Item number one.

(f)   Mein Name ist Annika. Ich bin 16 und ich habe seit sechs Monaten einen Teilzeitjob. Ich arbeite in einem kleinen Supermarkt um die Ecke. Ich arbeite meistens an der Kasse, aber wir müssen auch jeden Abend die Regale auffüllen.

Ich arbeite donnerstags nach der Schule von sechs Uhr bis halb neun und samstags von acht Uhr bis halb fünf, also elf Stunden pro Woche. Ich verdiene €6,50 pro Stunde. Ich glaube, dass die Arbeit gut bezahlt ist.

Aber die Arbeit gefällt mir gar nicht: Die Mitarbeiter sind freundlich und hilfsbereit, aber es ist eine anstrengende Arbeit und so langweilig, weil ich so lange sitzen muss. Ich bekomme kein Taschengeld von meinen Eltern, aber ich verdiene ja ungefähr siebzig Euro die Woche.

Um etwas extra zu verdienen, muss ich bei der Hausarbeit helfen. Ich helfe meinem Vater beim Autowaschen und nach dem Abendessen muss ich die Spülmaschine einräumen und auch ausräumen. Ich finde das fair, weil meine Eltern ja beide arbeiten müssen.

(2 minutes)

(t) Item number two.

Annika continues in an interview.

You now have one minute to study the questions for Item number two.

(m) Annika, in welche Klasse gehst du?

(f) Ich bin im Moment in meinem letzten Jahr auf dem Immanuel-Kant-Gymnasium hier in Königsberg.

(m) Gehst du gern in die Schule?

(f) Oh ja, natürlich, aber ich muss sehr früh aufstehen, um Viertel vor sieben, weil die Schule um fünf vor acht anfängt. Daher nehme ich den Bus um Viertel nach sieben.

(m) Und um wie viel Uhr ist die Schule aus?

(f) Um halb eins, aber nachmittags haben wir AGs, das sind Arbeitsgemeinschaften: Bensu, eine Freundin aus meiner Klasse, und ich gehen zum Schulorchester, wo wir beide Geige spielen.

(m) Wie viele Fächer hast du dieses Jahr?

(f) Viele! Dieses Jahr habe ich Mathe, Englisch, Französisch, Italienisch und Deutsch, natürlich.

(m) Was! Drei Fremdsprachen?

(f) Ja, genau. Drei Fremdsprachen. Ich interessiere mich sehr für Fremdsprachen. Französisch ist mein bestes Fach: Ich glaube, dass ich motiviert bin, und ich arbeite, so gut ich kann. Und ich komme auch gut mit dem Lehrer aus: Er hat viel Geduld mit uns und hat einen guten Sinn für Humor.

(m) Und dein schlechtestes Fach?

(f) Das war letztes Jahr Geschichte. Kein Zweifel. Ich fand Geschichte schwierig und ich konnte mich im Unterricht nicht richtig konzentrieren.

(m) Hast du Pläne für die Zukunft?

(f) Ich weiß es noch nicht. Meine beste Freundin, Lara, war mit der Schule nicht zufrieden und hat dieses Jahr mit 16 die Schule verlassen. Sie hat einen Job bei einem Tierarzt gefunden und arbeitet jetzt mit Tieren.

(m) Planst du, auf die Uni zu gehen?

(f) Ja. Ich möchte vielleicht Englisch und Französisch an der Uni studieren.

(m) Wo?

(f) Keine Ahnung, aber nach Abschluss des Studiums hoffe ich, ein Gap-Year zu machen, vielleicht in Australien oder Neuseeland. Mein Traum wäre ein Job mit Kindern in einem Kindergarten oder in einer Grundschule . . .

(m) Das ist eine schöne Idee, Annika. Danke.

(f) Bitte sehr.

(2 minutes)

(t) End of test.

Now look over your answers.

[END OF TRANSCRIPT]

Page three

[BLANK PAGE]

DO NOT WRITE ON THIS PAGE

NATIONAL 5

2015

N5

National Qualifications 2015

Mark

X734/75/01

German Reading

TUESDAY, 26 MAY

9:00 AM — 10:30 AM

Fill in these boxes and read what is printed below.

Full name of centre

Town

Forename(s)

Surname

Number of seat

Date of birth

Day	Month	Year	Scottish candidate number

Total marks — 30

Attempt ALL questions.

Write your answers clearly, in **English**, in the spaces provided in this booklet.

You may use a German dictionary.

Additional space for answers is provided at the end of this booklet. If you use this space you must clearly identify the question number you are attempting.

Use **blue** or **black** ink.

There is a separate question and answer booklet for Writing. You must complete your answer for Writing in the question and answer booklet for Writing.

Before leaving the examination room you must give both booklets to the Invigilator; if you do not, you may lose all the marks for this paper.

MARKS | DO NOT WRITE IN THIS MARGIN

Total marks — 30

Attempt ALL questions

Text 1

This passage is about exam stress and how to overcome this.

Prüfungsangst — dieses Gefühl, das jeder kennt. Viele Leute zittern, wenn sie das Wort „Prüfung" hören.

Wenn man sich auf eine Prüfung gut vorbereiten will, sollte man die Zeit gut planen. Man sollte zum Beispiel nicht stundenlang am Schreibtisch sitzen — eine kleine Pause alle neunzig Minuten ist die beste Belohnung.

Laura, 16, ist Schülerin am Schiller-Gymnasium in Hamburg: „Vor einer Prüfung habe ich meistens schwitzige Hände und habe keinen Appetit mehr. Wenn ich etwas lernen muss, schreibe ich eine Frage auf eine Karte und auf die Rückseite kommt dann die Antwort. Wenn ich eine mündliche Prüfung habe, übe ich mit einer Freundin. Das machen wir in einer neuen Umgebung, vielleicht in einem Café in der Stadt oder in der Schulbibliothek."

Lars Ritter ist Direktor der Rhein-Schule in Köln und er kennt die Sorgen, die Schüler in der Prüfungszeit erleben: „Wir sagen den Schülern, dass Prüfungsangst normal und sogar nötig ist. Ohne Angst würde man die Prüfungssituation nicht ernst nehmen. Negative Gedanken so wie: ‚Durchfallen wäre eine Katastrophe', muss man vergessen. Viel besser ist es, wenn man denkt: ‚Ich habe mich auf die Prüfung vorbereitet und ich hoffe, dass ich eine gute Note bekomme.'"

Questions

(a) How do many people react to the mention of exams? Complete the following sentence.

      1

Lots of people _____ when they hear the word "exam".

(b) What is the best way to plan your time for studying? Give **two** details.

      2

_____

_____

MARKS | DO NOT WRITE IN THIS MARGIN

Text 1 Questions (continued)

(c) How does Laura react before exams? State any **one** thing.   1

_____

(d)   (i) How does she prepare for **speaking** exams?   1

_____

      (ii) Where does she do this? State any **one** thing.   1

_____

(e) What does headmaster Lars Ritter say to his pupils about exam nerves?
     State **two** things.   2

_____

_____

(f) Lars Ritter gives examples of the negative and positive thoughts students
     can have about exams.

      (i) Which negative thought does he mention?   1

_____

      (ii) Give **one** of the positive thoughts students might have.   1

_____

[Turn over

MARKS | DO NOT WRITE IN THIS MARGIN

Text 2

Lisa Wiedermann recently visited India and spent time at an international school.

Im Februar dieses Jahres hatte ich die Gelegenheit, mit einer Gruppe nach Indien zu fahren. Die Organisation „Asien-Kontakt" hat die Hälfte meiner Reisekosten bezahlt. Diese Organisation will Kontakt zwischen Jugendlichen in Indien und Deutschland fördern — sowie auch Toleranz zwischen den beiden Ländern.

An meinem ersten Tag in der indischen Schule habe ich eine schöne Blumenkette bekommen — das ist ein Zeichen der Freundschaft. Wir hatten natürlich auch Geschenke und Infomaterial aus Deutschland mitgebracht.

Ich war sehr beeindruckt von der Gastfreundlichkeit unserer indischen Gastgeber. Sie haben so viele Ausflüge für uns organisiert, um uns das Land und Leute näher zu bringen, jeden Abend gab es ein richtiges Fest mit indischen Spezialitäten und wir haben sogar das indische Parlamentsgebäude in Neu Delhi besucht.

Für mich war es erstaunlich, dass sich so viele Leute in Indien für Deutschland und die Deutschen interessieren. In der Schule zeigten uns zwei Schülerinnen die Bücher, die sie ganz auf Deutsch gelesen hatten. Drei Jungen erzählten uns über die zwei Wochen, die sie bei einer Kirchengruppe in Hamburg verbracht hatten.

Nächstes Jahr möchte ich mit meiner Familie zurückfahren, um dieses schöne Land besser kennen zu lernen.

Questions

(a) In what way did the organisation *Asien-Kontakt* help Lisa Wiedermann?   1

_____

_____

MARKS | DO NOT WRITE IN THIS MARGIN

Text 2 Questions (continued)

(b) What does this organisation want to promote? State **two** things.

2

_____

_____

(c) Why was Lisa given a necklace of flowers on her first day at the Indian school?

1

_____

_____

(d) Lisa was impressed by Indian hospitality.

What did the Indian hosts arrange for the German visitors? State **three** things.

3

_____

_____

_____

(e) What showed Lisa that Indian people have an interest in Germany?

Complete the sentences.

2

Two pupils showed her books which _____

_____.

Three boys told her about _____

_____.

(f) Reading the passage as a whole, why do you think Lisa has chosen to write it?

Tick (✓) the correct box.

1

She wants to move to India when she is older.	
She wants to promote understanding between the two countries.	
She wants to promote India as a holiday destination.	

MARKS | DO NOT WRITE IN THIS MARGIN

Text 3

Sara, a German girl, is writing about her work placement and how to plan for the future.

Meine Lehrer in der Schule haben mir bei meiner Berufswahl sehr geholfen. Sie haben mit mir und meinen Eltern gesprochen, denn sie wissen, dass meine Noten in der Schule nicht immer gut sind. Sie sagen aber, dass ich eine gute Schülerin bin und das finde ich toll. Ich habe ein Arbeitspraktikum in einer Bäckerei gemacht und das hat großen Spaß gemacht. Die Arbeit ist sehr kreativ, man kann mit den Händen arbeiten, was ich sehr gut finde, und man kann auch mit neuen Ideen experimentieren. Als ich mein Praktikum machte, hatte ich eine gute Idee für einen Weihnachtskuchen und mein Chef hat gesagt: „Ja, warum nicht?" Mein Kuchen hat sehr gut geschmeckt und sie haben ihn in der Konditorei verkauft. Ich war so stolz.

Schon in der Schulzeit sollte man an eine künftige Karriere denken. Das ist nicht immer so einfach, denn man hat oft andere, wichtigere Dinge zu tun, wie zum Beispiel Prüfungen ablegen oder neue Talente entdecken und entwickeln. Viele Schüler fühlen sich einfach zu jung und unerfahren, um an ihre Berufswahl zu denken.

Ein Arbeitspraktikum ist aber eine gute Möglichkeit, Einblicke in die Arbeitswelt zu bekommen. Man kann durch eigene Erfahrung lernen und persönliche Kontakte schließen.

Questions

(a) Which of the following statements best describes Sara's work in school?

Tick (✓) the **one** correct statement. 1

Sara works well in school and is a high achiever.	
Sara's work is not perfect but she is a good pupil.	

(b) Why did Sara enjoy her work placement in the bakery? Give **three** reasons. 3

_____

_____

_____

MARKS | DO NOT WRITE IN THIS MARGIN

Text 3 Questions (continued)

(c) Why was Sarah proud of her Christmas cake? State **two** things.

2

_____

_____

(d) What is often more important to school pupils than thinking about a future career? State **two** things.

2

_____

_____

(e) There are many advantages of doing a work placement. State any **two** of these.

2

_____

_____

[END OF QUESTION PAPER]

ADDITIONAL SPACE FOR ANSWERS

Page eight

MARKS | DO NOT WRITE IN THIS MARGIN

ADDITIONAL SPACE FOR ANSWERS

Page nine

[BLANK PAGE]

DO NOT WRITE ON THIS PAGE

N5

National Qualifications 2015

Mark

X734/75/02

German Writing

TUESDAY, 26 MAY
9:00 AM – 10:30 AM

Fill in these boxes and read what is printed below.

Full name of centre

Town

Forename(s)

Surname

Number of seat

Date of birth

Day	Month	Year	Scottish candidate number

Total marks — 20

Write your answer clearly, in **German**, in the space provided in this booklet.

You may use a German dictionary.

Additional space for answers is provided at the end of this booklet.

Use **blue** or **black** ink.

There is a separate question and answer booklet for Reading. You must complete your answers for Reading in the question and answer booklet for Reading.

Before leaving the examination room you must give both booklets to the Invigilator; if you do not, you may lose all the marks for this paper.

Total marks — 20

You are preparing an application for the job advertised below and you write an e-mail in **German** to the company.

Hotel „Sonnenhof"

Annagasse 15 — 90402 Nürnberg

Die Leitung des Hotels „Sonnenhof" sucht sofort freundliche, motivierte, junge Leute als

Mitarbeiter/-innen an der Hotelrezeption

Sie sollten gute Sprachkenntnisse in Englisch und Deutsch haben und sollten gut mit unseren Gästen umgehen können.

Sie können uns unter info@hotel-sonnenhof.de für weitere Information kontaktieren und uns Ihre Bewerbung schicken.

Ihre Bewerbung sollte folgende Information enthalten:

To help you to write your e-mail, you have been given the following checklist.

You must include **all** of these points:

- Personal details (name, age, where you live)
- School/college/education experience until now
- Skills/interests you have which make you right for the job
- Related work experience
- Any links you may have with a German-speaking country
- Your future education/career plans

Use all of the above to help you write the e-mail in **German**. The e-mail should be approximately 120–150 words. You may use a German dictionary.

ANSWER SPACE

MARKS DO NOT WRITE IN THIS MARGIN

ANSWER SPACE (continued)

MARKS DO NOT WRITE IN THIS MARGIN

ANSWER SPACE (continued)

MARKS DO NOT WRITE IN THIS MARGIN

ANSWER SPACE (continued)

[END OF QUESTION PAPER]

MARKS | DO NOT WRITE IN THIS MARGIN

ADDITIONAL SPACE FOR ANSWERS

MARKS | DO NOT WRITE IN THIS MARGIN

ADDITIONAL SPACE FOR ANSWERS

N5

National
Qualifications
2015

Mark

X734/75/03

**German
Listening**

TUESDAY, 26 MAY

10:50 AM – 11:15 AM (approx)

Fill in these boxes and read what is printed below.

Full name of centre

Town

Forename(s)

Surname

Number of seat

Date of birth

Day	Month	Year	Scottish candidate number

Total marks — 20

Attempt ALL questions.

You will hear two items in German. **Before you hear each item, you will have one minute to study the questions.** You will hear each item three times, with an interval of one minute between playings. You will then have time to answer the questions before hearing the next item.

You may NOT use a German dictionary.

Write your answers clearly, in **English**, in the spaces provided in this booklet. Additional space for answers is provided at the end of this booklet. If you use this space you must clearly identify the question number you are attempting.

Use **blue** or **black** ink.

You are not allowed to leave the examination room until the end of the test.

Before leaving the examination room you must give this booklet to the Invigilator; if you do not, you may lose all the marks for this paper.

MARKS | DO NOT WRITE IN THIS MARGIN

Total marks — 20

Attempt ALL questions

Item 1

Erik is talking about life at home and why he has two bedrooms.

(a) When is Erik's birthday? Tick (✓) the correct box.   **1**

3rd August	
13th August	
31st August	

(b) When did Erik's parents separate?   **1**

_____

_____

(c) When does Erik live with his father? State any **two** things.   **2**

_____

_____

(d) What are the arrangements for Erik at Christmas? State **two** things.   **2**

_____

_____

(e) Why is Maths Erik's favourite subject?   **1**

_____

_____

(f) Overall, how does Erik feel about life at the moment?
Tick (✓) the most appropriate statement.   **1**

He is unhappy.	
He has his ups and downs.	
He is positive.	

Item 2

Erik continues in an interview.

(a) Who is Martin?   1

_____

(b) What does he say about his relationship with Martin?
State any **one** thing.   1

_____

_____

(c) What do Erik's parents do for a living? Complete the grid.   2

Mother	
Father	

(d) Why can't Erik and Martin have a dog?   1

_____

_____

(e) (i) **Apart from** electric guitar, what instrument does Erik play?   1

_____

(ii) How long has he been playing this instrument?   1

_____

(f) What does Erik say about his friends at school? State any **three** things.   3

_____

_____

_____

(g) What do Erik and his friend do in their spare time? State any **two** things.   2

_____

_____

[END OF QUESTION PAPER]

ADDITIONAL SPACE FOR ANSWERS

MARKS

DO NOT WRITE IN THIS MARGIN

MARKS DO NOT WRITE IN THIS MARGIN

ADDITIONAL SPACE FOR ANSWERS

Page five

[BLANK PAGE]

DO NOT WRITE ON THIS PAGE

**National
Qualifications
2015**

X734/75/13

**German
Listening Transcript**

TUESDAY, 26 MAY

10:50 AM – 11:15 AM

This paper must not be seen by any candidate.

The material overleaf is provided for use in an emergency only (eg the recording or equipment proving faulty) or where permission has been given in advance by SQA for the material to be read to candidates with additional support needs. The material must be read exactly as printed.

Instructions to reader(s):

For each item, read the English once, then read the German **three times**, with an interval of 1 minute between the three readings. On completion of the third reading, pause for the length of time indicated in brackets after the item, to allow the candidates to write their answers.

Where special arrangements have been agreed in advance to allow the reading of the material, those sections marked **(f)** should be read by a female speaker and those marked **(m)** by a male; those sections marked **(t)** should be read by the teacher.

(t) **Item number one.**

Erik is talking about life at home and why he has two bedrooms.

You now have one minute to study the questions for Item number one.

(m) Mein Name ist Erik und ich bin 15. Ich habe am 13. August Geburtstag. Ich wohne in einem Haus in Nürnberg-Galgenhof — das ist ein Vorort von Nürnberg. Ich habe zwei Schlafzimmer, das eine bei meiner Mutter hier in Nürnberg und das zweite bei meinem Vater in Fürth. Fürth liegt nur acht Kilometer von Nürnberg entfernt.

Meine Eltern haben sich vor vier Jahren getrennt, als ich elf Jahre alt war. Ich lebe die meiste Zeit bei meiner Mutter. Aber mittwochs, jedes zweite Wochenende und vier Wochen in den Schulferien wohne ich bei meinem Vater und seiner Freundin.

Ich verbringe Weihnachten immer bei meiner Mutter. Meinen Vater besuche ich immer zwei Tage später. So bekomme ich zweimal Geschenke. Das ist toll!

Ich gehe in die zehnte Klasse eines Gymnasiums in Nürnberg. Am besten gefallen mir die Fächer Kunst, Musik und Mathe. Mathe ist mein Lieblingsfach und ich bekomme immer gute Noten. Und natürlich auch Sport! Außerdem spiele ich Fußball und Volleyball im Verein.

(2 minutes)

(t) Item number two.

Erik continues in an interview.

You now have one minute to study the questions for Item number two.

(f) Erik, hast du Geschwister?

(m) Ja, zu Hause sind wir zu dritt. Meine Mutter, mein kleiner Bruder Martin und ich. Martin ist zwei Jahre jünger als ich.

(f) Kommst du mit Martin gut aus?

(m) Ja, klar! Wir kommen miteinander ganz gut aus — er kann mir ab und zu auf die Nerven gehen, zum Beispiel, wenn er in mein Zimmer kommt, ohne an die Tür zu klopfen, aber ich mag ihn.

(f) Was machen deine Eltern beruflich?

(m) Meine Mutter ist Sekretärin in einem Büro in der Stadtmitte und mein Vater ist Polizist. Meine Mutter ist klein und schlank. Sie hat blonde Haare und grüne Augen. Mein Vater ist 42 und meine Mutter ist zwei Jahre jünger.

(f) Habt ihr Haustiere?

(m) Ja, wir haben zwei Goldfische. Martin und ich möchten sehr gerne einen Hund, aber meine Mutter ist gegen Hunde allergisch!

(f) Du interessierst dich für Musik. Spielst du ein Instrument?

(m) Ja, ich spiele seit drei Jahren Klavier und seit einem Jahr elektrische Gitarre. Ich gehe mit zwei Freunden zur Musikgruppe in der Stadtmitte, wo wir zusammen Musik machen.

(f) Hast du viele Freunde in der Schule?

(m) Ja, ich habe drei oder vier echt gute Freunde. Sie sind oft ziemlich laut, aber ich finde sie auch sehr lustig und wir haben die gleichen Interessen.

(f) Treibt ihr auch viel Sport?

(m) Ja, wir gehen zusammen im Stadtpark joggen, machen in der Gegend Radtouren und spielen in der Fußballmannschaft der Schule — ich bin Stürmer. Wir gehen auch regelmäßig ins Kino.

(f) Was für Filme seht ihr gerne?

(m) Wir sehen uns gern Abenteuerfilme an. Mein Lieblingsschauspieler ist Will Smith und mein Lieblingsfilm ist «X-Men».

(f) Danke, Erik!

(m) Kein Problem!

(2 minutes)

(t) End of test.

Now look over your answers.

[END OF TRANSCRIPT]

Page four

[BLANK PAGE]

DO NOT WRITE ON THIS PAGE

NATIONAL 5

2016

N5

National Qualifications 2016

X734/75/01

German Reading

Mark ☐

WEDNESDAY, 1 JUNE
1:00 PM – 2:30 PM

Fill in these boxes and read what is printed below.

Full name of centre

Town

Forename(s)

Surname

Number of seat

Date of birth

Day	Month	Year

Scottish candidate number

Total marks — 30

Attempt ALL questions.

Write your answers clearly, in **English**, in the spaces provided in this booklet.

You may use a German dictionary.

Additional space for answers is provided at the end of this booklet. If you use this space you must clearly identify the question number you are attempting.

Use **blue** or **black** ink.

There is a separate question and answer booklet for Writing. You must complete your answer for Writing in the question and answer booklet for Writing.

Before leaving the examination room you must give this booklet to the Invigilator; if you do not, you may lose all the marks for this paper.

Total marks — 30

Attempt ALL questions

Text 1

You read an online article explaining what citizens in Munich can do to help protect the environment.

Wie kann man als Bürger hier in München mehr für die Umwelt tun? Hier einige Tipps, wie man unseren Planeten schützen kann.

Kostenlose Zeitungen und unerwünschte Broschüren im Briefkasten bedeuten eine Verschwendung von Rohstoffen. Ein Aufkleber an der Haustür, der sagt „STOP — Bitte keine Werbung", ist eine billige und wirksame Lösung.

In München gibt es heute immer mehr Geschäfte, wo man Bio-Obst und -Gemüse kaufen kann. Hier muss man aber vorsichtig sein, denn Bio-Kiwis aus Neuseeland oder Bio-Äpfel aus Argentinien werden mit dem Flugzeug nach Deutschland transportiert und deswegen gibt es so viel Luftverschmutzung.

Wenn man etwas braucht, ist es nicht immer nötig, etwas Neues zu kaufen. Wenn man zum Beispiel einen neuen Tisch braucht, kann man einen alten Tisch auf einem Flohmarkt kaufen. Das sieht oft besser aus und ist normalerweise preiswerter.

Studenten an der Uni können sich oft gegenseitig helfen. Man kann zum Beispiel Kleider austauschen, und man kann andere Sachen wie Sportartikel teilen.

Es ist auch gut, wenn man versucht, kaputte Dinge zu reparieren. Wenn man ein Fahrrad oder eine Waschmaschine reparieren kann, ist das viel besser als etwas Neues zu kaufen. Jedes Jahr in Deutschland landen 500.000 Tonnen Elektrogeräte auf dem Schrotthaufen und das ist viel zu viel.

Questions

(a) What does the article say about junk mail? Complete the sentence.   1

Free newspapers and unwanted brochures are a waste of

_____ .

(b) What is a good and cheap way of stopping this junk mail?   1

_____

_____

MARKS | DO NOT WRITE IN THIS MARGIN

Text 1 Questions (continued)

(c) Why do you have to be careful when buying organic fruit from countries such as Argentina and New Zealand? State **two** things.   2

_____

_____

(d) What are the benefits of buying an old table instead of a brand new one? State **two** things.   2

_____

_____

(e) What can students at the university do to help? State **two** things.   2

_____

_____

(f) (i) There is a final suggestion on how to help the environment. What is this?   1

_____

_____

(ii) What statistic supports this suggestion at the end of the article? Complete the sentence.   1

500,000 tonnes of _____
land on the scrapheap each year.

[Turn over

MARKS | DO NOT WRITE IN THIS MARGIN

Text 2

You are browsing a German online magazine when the following article about an interesting school catches your eye.

Bis vor kurzem haben fast keine Schüler des Sophie Scholl Gymnasiums in München in der Schulkantine gegessen. Das Essen war wenig schmackhaft. Die Schüler gingen lieber in Fastfood-Restaurants, aber das Essen in diesen Restaurants enthält oft viel Fett.

Die Schüler haben aber eine Lösung zu diesem Problem gefunden: Sie kochen selbst jeden Tag. Alle zwei Wochen ist eine andere Klasse für das Mittagessen verantwortlich.

Der Schuldirektor findet das Projekt wichtig für die Gesundheit der Schüler. Die meisten Kinder haben ihre Essgewohnheiten geändert. Wenn sie abends nach Hause kommen, wird das Essen nicht mehr im Mikrowellenherd aufgewärmt. Die Schüler haben jetzt Lust, mit frischen Zutaten zu kochen.

Weil die Schüler so viel in der Schule machen müssen, lernen sie Verantwortung zu übernehmen. Sie lernen auch etwas über die Zusammenarbeit mit anderen und auch wie viel die Lebensmittel kosten.

Das Projekt hat viel Erfolg gehabt. Mehr Schüler essen jetzt in der Kantine. Das Schulessen ist jetzt lecker und viel gesünder. Es gibt noch einen Vorteil — die Schüler können eine zweite Portion kostenlos bekommen.

Questions

(a) What does the article say about eating habits at the Sophie Scholl Gymnasium? Complete the sentences.   2

Until recently _____ pupils ate in the school canteen.

The food was _____ .

(b) What solution have the pupils found to this problem? State **two** things.   2

_____

_____

MARKS | DO NOT WRITE IN THIS MARGIN

Text 2 Questions (continued)

(c) In what ways have eating habits for pupils changed at home? State **two** things.

_____

_____

(d) What have the pupils learned as a result of this project? State any **two** things.

_____

_____

(e) Give **two** reasons why more pupils are now eating in the canteen.

_____

_____

[Turn over

MARKS | DO NOT WRITE IN THIS MARGIN

Text 3

You read an article about starting your own business.

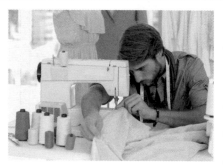

Heute wollen immer mehr Leute eine eigene Firma gründen. Das bringt sicher viele Vorteile mit sich — man kann immer das machen, was man will. Man ist selbst für Zeitmanagement verantwortlich und man hat die Chance, eigene Ideen zu entwickeln.

Manfred Schultz ist heute Inhaber einer kleinen Textilfirma. Die Idee hatte er, als er Student war: „Ich hatte begonnen, meine eigenen Kleider zu machen und ich habe sie auf dem Sonntagsmarkt in der Stadt verkauft. Sehr viele Studenten haben meine Kleider gekauft, und bald begann ich sie in der Stadt zu sehen. Das hat mich ermutigt, weiterzumachen!

Am Ende meiner Studienzeit hatte ich genug Geld für einen Gebrauchtwagen und für eine achtwöchige Reise durch ganz Italien. Später habe ich ein kleines Geschäft in meiner Heimatstadt eröffnet.

So einfach ist es aber nicht. Man muss an die Nebenkosten denken: Man braucht eine Versicherung und man muss oft eine Nähmaschine reparieren lassen.

Natürlich muss man auch mit Enttäuschungen rechnen. Viele Leute finden das schwierig. Ich hatte zum Beispiel gehofft, dass ein großes Warenhaus meine Kleider kaufen würde, aber am Ende wollten sie meine Jacken und Hemden verändern und das war für mich absolut inakzeptabel. Trotzdem bin ich immer noch zufrieden mit der Arbeit."

Questions

(a) According to the article, what are the advantages of starting your own business? State any **two** things.   2

_____

_____

(b) (i) Where did Manfred Schultz first sell the clothes he had made?   1

_____

(ii) What things encouraged him to keep going? State **two** things.   2

_____

_____

Page six

MARKS | DO NOT WRITE IN THIS MARGIN

Text 3 Questions (continued)

(c) What did Manfred do when his studies were finished? State any **two** things.

2

_____

_____

(d) There are many additional costs involved in running a business. Give any **one** example of these.

1

_____

(e) Why did Manfred reject the chance to have his designs in a big department store?

1

_____

(f) What general view does this article give of running your own business? Tick (✓) the correct box.

1

	Tick (✓)
It's something that anyone can do.	
It's worthwhile, although there are also difficulties.	
It's just not worth all the effort.	

[END OF QUESTION PAPER]

MARKS | DO NOT WRITE IN THIS MARGIN

ADDITIONAL SPACE FOR ANSWERS

MARKS | DO NOT WRITE IN THIS MARGIN

ADDITIONAL SPACE FOR ANSWERS

[BLANK PAGE]

DO NOT WRITE ON THIS PAGE

N5

National Qualifications 2016

Mark

X734/75/02

German Writing

WEDNESDAY, 1 JUNE
1:00 PM — 2:30 PM

Fill in these boxes and read what is printed below.

Full name of centre

Town

Forename(s)

Surname

Number of seat

Date of birth

Day   Month   Year

Scottish candidate number

Total marks — 20

Write your answer clearly, in **German**, in the space provided in this booklet.

You may use a German dictionary.

Additional space for answers is provided at the end of this booklet.

Use **blue** or **black** ink.

There is a separate question and answer booklet for Reading. You must complete your answers for Reading in the question and answer booklet for Reading.

Before leaving the examination room you must give this booklet to the Invigilator; if you do not, you may lose all the marks for this paper.

MARKS

Total marks — 20

You are preparing an application for the job advertised below and you write an e-mail in **German** to the company.

Gaststube "Rheinblick"

Flußweg 3,
55422 Bacharach,
Rheinland-Pfalz

Wir suchen für unser Restaurant **einen Kellner/eine Kellnerin.**

Sind Sie fleißig, motiviert und höflich?

Haben Sie gute Englisch- und Deutschkenntnisse?

Schicken Sie Ihre Bewerbung an:

info@gaststube.rheinblick.de

To help you to write your e-mail, you have been given the following checklist.
You must include **all** of these points:

- Personal details (name, age, where you live)
- School/college/education experience until now
- Skills/interests you have which make you right for the job
- Related work experience
- Any previous links with Germany or a German-speaking country
- Any questions related to the job

Use all of the above to help you write the e-mail in **German**. The e-mail should be approximately 120–150 words. You may use a German dictionary.

MARKS

ANSWER SPACE

ANSWER SPACE (continued)

ANSWER SPACE (continued)

MARKS | DO NOT WRITE IN THIS MARGIN

ANSWER SPACE (continued)

[END OF QUESTION PAPER]

MARKS DO NOT WRITE IN THIS MARGIN

ADDITIONAL SPACE FOR ANSWERS

Page seven

ADDITIONAL SPACE FOR ANSWERS

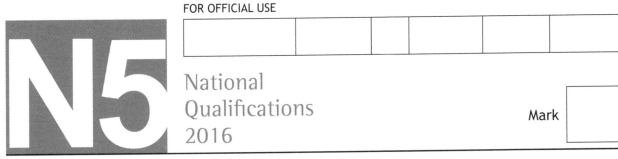

N5

National Qualifications 2016

X734/75/03

Mark

German Listening

WEDNESDAY, 1 JUNE

2:50 PM — 3:20 PM (approx)

Fill in these boxes and read what is printed below.

Full name of centre

Town

Forename(s)

Surname

Number of seat

Date of birth

Day	Month	Year

Scottish candidate number

Total marks — 20

Attempt ALL questions.

You will hear two items in German. **Before you hear each item, you will have one minute to study the questions.** You will hear each item three times, with an interval of one minute between playings. You will then have time to answer the questions before hearing the next item.

You may NOT use a German dictionary.

Write your answers clearly, in **English**, in the spaces provided in this booklet. Additional space for answers is provided at the end of this booklet. If you use this space you must clearly identify the question number you are attempting.

Use **blue** or **black** ink.

You are not allowed to leave the examination room until the end of the test.

Before leaving the examination room you must give this booklet to the Invigilator; if you do not, you may lose all the marks for this paper.

MARKS | DO NOT WRITE IN THIS MARGIN

Total marks — 20

Attempt ALL questions

Item 1

Evelyn Hirsch, from Hamburg, is talking about spending holidays with friends.

(a) What kind of accommodation do people choose when on holiday with friends? State any **two** things.

2

_____

_____

(b) Evelyn gives various reasons for spending holidays with friends. State any **one** of these.

1

_____

(c) Where exactly did Evelyn and her husband rent a villa last year with their friends?

1

_____

(d) Where did they find the accommodation?

1

_____

(e) What does Evelyn enjoy doing on holiday? State any **two** things.

2

_____

_____

(f) What is Evelyn's personal view on holidays with friends? Tick (✓) the correct statement.

1

	Tick (✓)
It's the only way to get the most out of a holiday.	
She's tried it and won't do it again.	
She's looking forward to doing it again.	

MARKS | DO NOT WRITE IN THIS MARGIN

Item 2

Evelyn and her husband Rolf are discussing their plans for this year's holiday.

(a) Why does Rolf want to go on holiday to Italy? Complete the following sentence.

1

Rolf wants to go to Italy because _____ recommended it to him.

(b) What reasons does Evelyn give for wanting to stay in Germany for the holidays? State any **two**.

2

_____

_____

(c) Why does Rolf not want to spend a holiday in a town? Give any **one** reason.

1

_____

(d) Where in Germany does Evelyn suggest that they could spend this year's holiday?

1

_____

(e) Why does Rolf not want to go there? State any **one** reason.

1

_____

(f) Why does Rolf suggest a holiday in Austria? Complete the following sentences.

2

Rolf wants to go to Austria because _____ .

It's beautiful and _____ .

(g) What puts Evelyn off going to Austria this year? State any **one** thing.

1

_____

(h) Rolf says Edinburgh is a wonderful place. Why else does he want to go there?

1

_____

[Turn over

MARKS

DO NOT
WRITE IN
THIS
MARGIN

Item 2 (continued)

(i)   Where do they finally decide to spend this year's holiday?   1

_____

(j)   What job will they do while on holiday?   1

_____

[END OF QUESTION PAPER]

MARKS | DO NOT WRITE IN THIS MARGIN

ADDITIONAL SPACE FOR ANSWERS

Page five

MARKS | DO NOT WRITE IN THIS MARGIN

ADDITIONAL SPACE FOR ANSWERS

National Qualifications 2016

X734/75/13

German
Listening Transcript

WEDNESDAY, 1 JUNE
2:50 PM — 3:20 PM (approx)

This paper must not be seen by any candidate.

The material overleaf is provided for use in an emergency only (eg the recording or equipment proving faulty) or where permission has been given in advance by SQA for the material to be read to candidates with additional support needs. The material must be read exactly as printed.

Instructions to reader(s):

For each item, read the English once, then read the German **three times**, with an interval of
1 minute between the three playings. On completion of the third reading, pause for the length of time indicated in brackets after the item, to allow the candidates to write their answers.

Where special arrangements have been agreed in advance to allow the reading of the material, those sections marked **(f)** should be read by a female speaker and those marked **(m)** by a male; those sections marked **(t)** should be read by the teacher.

(t) **Item Number One**

Evelyn Hirsch, from Hamburg, is talking about spending holidays with friends.

You now have one minute to study the questions for Item Number One.

(f) Sehr viele Deutsche fahren jedes Jahr in den Urlaub und Millionen von uns verbringen gern Ferien mit Freunden. Wir mieten ein Strandhaus auf Korfu, eine Ferienwohnung in Spanien oder wir verbringen Zeit in einem Wohnwagen in den Alpen.

Ja, solche Ferien mit Freunden sind sehr beliebt und es gibt viele Gründe dafür: Man kann zusammenwohnen und die Arbeit teilen, zum Beispiel das Kochen und Abwaschen. Es ist viel billiger als im Hotel und viele Leute haben Freunde, die vielleicht eine andere Sprache sprechen können. Für uns war es aber ganz anders.

Mein Mann und ich sind letztes Jahr nach Südfrankreich gefahren und wir haben eine Ferienvilla mit unseren Freunden Lars und Annette geteilt. Die Villa haben wir in einer Ferienbroschüre gefunden. Von Anfang an war es eine absolute Katastrophe.

Im Urlaub liege ich sehr gern in der Sonne, schwimme im Meer oder ich gehe gern ins große Einkaufszentrum in der nächsten Stadt. Mein Mann Rolf verbringt am liebsten Zeit in der Kunstgalerie. Letztes Jahr konnten wir das nicht machen, weil unsere Freunde auch da waren. Nächstes Jahr fahren wir allein in den Urlaub.

(2 minutes)

(t)   **Item Number Two**

Evelyn and her husband Rolf are discussing their plans for this year's holiday.

You now have one minute to study the questions for Item Number Two.

(m)   Ich möchte dieses Jahr die Ferien in Italien verbringen. Meine Chefin war letztes Jahr da und sie meint, dass das Land sehr schön sei, und die Leute sehr freundlich.

(f)   Schon gut Rolf, aber Ferien im Ausland sind nicht immer was für mich. Man kann auch hier in Deutschland bleiben und gute Ferien haben. Man kann überall mit dem Auto hinfahren und man kann das Land besser kennen lernen.

(m)   Ich will unter keinen Umständen meine Ferien in einer Stadt verbringen. Im Urlaub will ich Hektik und Stress vergessen. Für mich ist die Ruhe sehr wichtig.

(f)   Ja, vielleicht hast du Recht. Wie wär's mit einem kleinen Ferienhaus an der Nordseeküste?

(m)   Nee. Das ist auch keine gute Idee. Du weißt ja, dass das Wetter da oft furchtbar ist. Ich war letztes Jahr in Norddeutschland und es hat die ganze Zeit geregnet.

(f)   Ja gut, dann ist ein Urlaub in der Stadt perfekt, weil es immer viel zu tun gibt, auch wenn das Wetter nicht gut ist.

(m)   Wir könnten einen Kompromiss finden. Warum fahren wir nicht nach Österreich? Es ist nicht zu weit weg, die Landschaft ist wunderschön, und so teuer ist es auch nicht. Was meinst du?

(f)   Österreich ist sicher ein sehr schönes Land, aber ich will da nicht hinfahren. Ich war vor zwei Jahren mit meiner Schwester da. Es war ganz gut, aber ich will etwas Neues erleben. Hast du vergessen?

(m)   Wir könnten vielleicht eine Woche in Schottland verbringen. Edinburg soll eine wunderbare Stadt sein, und die Einkaufsmöglichkeiten sind super.

(f)   Aber Rolf, du wolltest doch keine Stadtferien. Edinburg ist ja die Hauptstadt von Schottland und es gibt sicher viele Touristen im Sommer da.

(m)   Mmm, vielleicht hast du Recht Evelyn. Ich glaube, wir werden dieses Jahr zu Hause bleiben. Wir können dadurch Geld sparen und wir müssen endlich die Zeit finden, die Garage aufzuräumen.

(2 minutes)

(t)   **End of test.**

Now look over your answers.

[END OF TRANSCRIPT]

[BLANK PAGE]

DO NOT WRITE ON THIS PAGE

NATIONAL 5

Answers

NATIONAL 5 GERMAN 2014

Reading

Text 1

(a) *Any two from:*
- Work <u>with a teacher in a small group</u>
- Discuss (their) <u>work</u> (with other pupils/teachers)
- Develop/improve their talents/ideas

(b) *Any two from:*
- You can <u>plan</u> (things) <u>better</u>
- You have (much more) freedom
- You learn to be independent

(c) (i) She was (a little) shy/she never said anything (in a normal class)

    (ii) • She has got to know (all pupils in) her <u>group</u>
- She isn't <u>afraid</u> to give/state her opinion

(d) *Any two from:*
- Appearance/the way you look/your look matters/is important
- To <u>keep/maintain/make</u> (better) eye contact
- To speak <u>more</u> slowly/<u>more</u> clearly

(e) Tick at **BOX 3**:
Pupils who like working with others ✓

Text 2

(a) People/Humans going to the cinema/the number of cinema visitors/people going through/to the door(s)

(b) Any one from:
- The (inter(national)) credit crunch/financial crisis/credit crisis/economic crisis
- <u>Many</u>/(many) <u>people</u> have less/not enough/little money (at their disposal)

(c) • They have enough parking spaces (for everyone)/Plenty of parking
- <u>Tickets</u> on special offer <u>twice a week/2 days a week</u>
- A (10%) discount for <u>regular visitors/regulars</u>

(d) • (More and more) people have <u>big(ger)</u> screens/<u>big(ger)</u> screen TVs/<u>big(ger)</u> TVs
- You can pause the film/it (when you want)
- You can download/watch the <u>latest/newest/new</u>/(most) recent films/hits

(e) • <u>Seven German</u> films were made/appeared/opened (in 3D) <u>last year</u>
- More than any country except the USA

Text 3

(a) Tick at **BOXES 2** and **3**:
- Washing clothes
- Showering

(b) • Well/fountain
- River/burn

(c) • Dirty water/it leads to/carries (serious/bad) illness(es)/disease(s)/can make you sick/ill
- (Can often be) fatal/deadly

(d) • (German) factories/industry <u>use(s)</u> <u>a lot</u>/<u>quantities of</u> <u>chemicals</u>/<u>chemical</u> products
- The chemicals/they are (sometimes) poisonous/flow into the rivers (Please ensure that 'they' refers to a mention of chemicals in previous bullet point)

(e) *Any two from:*
- Water the plants/garden (no more than) once a week/(only) once a week
- Don't leave the tap running/Turn the tap off
- (Only) switch on/use the dishwasher when it is full

Writing

General Marking Principles

Candidates will write a piece of extended writing in the modern language by addressing six bullet points. These bullet points will follow on from a job-related scenario. The bullet points will cover the four contexts of society, learning, employability and culture to allow candidates to use and adapt learned material. The first four bullet points will be the same each year and the last two will change to suit the scenario. Candidates need to address these "unpredictable bullet points" in detail to access the full range of marks.

Category	Mark	Content	Accuracy	Language resource – variety, range, structures
Very good	20	The job advert has been addressed in a full and balanced way. The candidate uses detailed language. The candidate addresses the advert completely and competently, **including information in response to both unpredictable bullet points.** A range of verbs/verb forms, tenses and constructions is used. Overall this comes over as a competent, well thought-out and serious application for the job.	The candidate handles all aspects of grammar and spelling accurately, although the language may contain one or two minor errors. Where the candidate attempts to use language more appropriate to Higher, a slightly higher number of inaccuracies need not detract from the overall very good impression.	The candidate is comfortable with the first person of the verb and generally uses a different verb in each sentence. Some modal verbs and infinitives may be used. There is good use of adjectives, adverbs and prepositional phrases and, where appropriate, word order. There may be a range of tenses. The candidate uses co-ordinating conjunctions and/or subordinate clauses where appropriate. The language of the e-mail flows well.
Good	16	The job advert has been addressed competently. There is less evidence of detailed language. The candidate uses a reasonable range of verbs/verb forms. Overall, the candidate has produced a genuine, reasonably accurate attempt at applying for the specific job, **even though he/she may not address one of the unpredictable bullet points.**	The candidate handles a range of verbs fairly accurately. There are some errors in spelling, adjective endings and, where relevant, case endings. Use of accents is less secure, where appropriate. Where the candidate is attempting to use more complex vocabulary and structures, these may be less successful, although basic structures are used accurately. There may be one or two examples of inaccurate dictionary use, especially in the unpredictable bullet points.	There may be repetition of verbs. There may be examples of listing, in particular when referring to school/college experience, without further amplification. There may be one or two examples of a co-ordinating conjunction, but most sentences are simple sentences. The candidate keeps to more basic vocabulary, particularly in response to either or both unpredictable bullet points.

Category	Mark	Content	Accuracy	Language resource — variety, range, structures
Satisfactory	12	The job advert has been addressed fairly competently. The candidate makes limited use of detailed language. The language is fairly repetitive and uses a limited range of verbs and fixed phrases, e.g. *I like, I go, I play*. The candidate copes fairly well with areas of personal details, education, skills, interests and work experience but does not deal fully with the two unpredictable bullet points **and indeed may not address either or both of the unpredictable bullet points.** On balance however the candidate has produced a satisfactory job application in the specific language.	The verbs are generally correct, but may be repetitive. There are quite a few errors in other parts of speech — gender of nouns, cases, singular/plural confusion, for instance. Prepositions may be missing, e.g. *I go the town.* Overall, there is more correct than incorrect.	The candidate copes with the first and third person of a few verbs, where appropriate. A limited range of verbs is used. Sentences are basic and mainly brief. There is minimal use of adjectives, probably mainly after *is* e.g. *Chemistry is interesting*. The candidate has a weak knowledge of plurals. There may be several spelling errors, e.g. reversal of vowel combinations.
Unsatisfactory	8	The job advert has been addressed in an uneven manner and/or with insufficient use of detailed language. The language is repetitive, e.g. *I like, I go, I play* may feature several times. There may be little difference between Satisfactory and Unsatisfactory. **Either or both of the unpredictable bullet points may not have been addressed.** There may be one sentence which is not intelligible to a sympathetic native speaker.	Ability to form tenses is inconsistent. There are errors in many other parts of speech — gender of nouns, cases, singular/plural confusion, for instance. Several errors are serious, perhaps showing mother tongue interference. The detail in the unpredictable bullet points may be very weak. Overall, there is more incorrect than correct.	The candidate copes mainly only with the personal language required in bullet points 1 and 2. The verbs *is* and *study* may also be used correctly. Sentences are basic. An English word may appear in the writing. There may be an example of serious dictionary misuse.

Category	Mark	Content	Accuracy	Language resource — variety, range, structures
Poor	4	The candidate has had considerable difficulty in addressing the job advert. There is little evidence of the use of detailed language. Three or four sentences may not be understood by a sympathetic native speaker. **Either or both of the unpredictable bullet points may not have been addressed.**	Many of the verbs are incorrect. There are many errors in other parts of speech — personal pronouns, gender of nouns, cases, singular/plural confusion, prepositions, for instance. The language is probably inaccurate throughout the writing.	The candidate cannot cope with more than one or two basic verbs. The candidate displays almost no knowledge of the present tense of verbs. Verbs used more than once may be written differently on each occasion. Sentences are very short. The candidate has a very limited vocabulary. Several English words may appear in the writing. There are examples of serious dictionary misuse.
Very poor	0	The candidate is unable to address the job advert. **The two unpredictable bullet points may not have been addressed.** Very little is intelligible to a sympathetic native speaker.	Virtually nothing is correct.	The candidate may only cope with the verbs *to have* and *to be*. Very few words are written correctly in the modern language. English words are used. There may be several examples of mother tongue interference. There may be several examples of serious dictionary misuse.

Listening

Item 1

(a) Six months/half a year

(b) *Any one from:*
- (She works mostly) on the till/checkout/Scans the items (for customers)/(Works as) a cashier
- (She has to) fill/stack/refill/restock the <u>shelves</u> (every evening)

(c) (0)4.30 (pm)/16.30/half four

(d) (i) €6.50

(ii) (It is) well paid/(It's) good pay/(It is) good/a good amount

(e) *Any one from:*
- friendly
- helpful

(f) *Any one from:*
- She doesn't like it
- (It's) tiring
- (It's) (so/very) boring
- She has to sit for a long time

(g) Tick at **BOX 1**:
about how she works part-time and also manages to help out at home.

Item 2

(a) <u>Last</u>/<u>final</u> year

(b) 6.45 (am)/quarter to seven

(c) *Any one from:*
- (Go to) clubs/(school) orchestra
- Plays the <u>violin</u>

(d) That she <u>does/studies/learns/has/takes three</u> <u>foreign</u>/<u>other</u> languages/French, Italian and English

(e) Ticks at **BOX 2** and **BOX 4**
- She is motivated in French.
- She works as well as she can.

(f) • She found it difficult/hard
- She couldn't concentrate (properly in the lesson)

(g) *Any two from:*
- Lara/She wasn't satisfied/happy/content at school
- She left school <u>at 16</u>/<u>this year</u>
- She has found a job at/in a vet's
- She is/enjoys working with animals (now)

(h) • (She hopes to do) a gap year/(She hopes to) go to/visit/spend time in Australia or/and New Zealand (Both countries must be mentioned)
- (Her dream job would) be/work with children/Be/work in a nursery/kindergarten/(primary) school/be a nursery teacher

Reading

Text 1

(a) *Accept any one of:* Shiver/quiver/tremble/shake/quake

(b) • Do not sit (at a desk) <u>for hours</u>
- (Take) a break/pause <u>every 90 minutes/every hour and a half/after 90 minutes</u>

(c) *Any one from:*
- Her <u>hands</u> sweat/she has sweaty <u>hands</u>
- She loses her appetite/has no appetite/can't eat

(d) (i) (She practises/works on/does/goes over/prepares) it with a/her <u>friend</u>

NB: insist on **friend (singular)**

(ii) *Any one from:*
- They do it in a new environment/surroundings/place
- in a café <u>in town/in the city</u>
- the <u>school</u> library

(e) • (Exam nerves are) normal/necessary

(one adjective is sufficient)

NB: Exam nerves are normal and necessary would only be awarded   **1 mark**

- Without fear/worry you wouldn't take it/them seriously/Without stress, your exams would not come first

NB: "Fear of exams is normal or you wouldn't take it seriously" should be awarded   **2 marks**

(f) (i) <u>Failing</u> (the exam) would be/is a <u>disaster/catastrophe</u>

(ii) *Any one from:*
- I (have) prepared/worked (for the exam)
- I hope/aim/plan to get (a) good grade(s)/mark(s)/result(s)/I will do well

NB: Insist on future intention

Text 2

(a) They paid <u>half</u> of her <u>travel/trip/journey</u> (costs)

(b) • Contact <u>between young people/teenagers in India and Germany</u>
- Tolerance between <u>the</u> (two) <u>countries/between India and Germany/both lands</u>

(c) As a sign/symbol/gesture of friendship/to show friendship/to mark her friendship

(d) *Any three from:*
- (Lots of) outings/trips/excursions
- <u>Every evening/night/in the evening</u> there was a celebration/party/festival
- There was Indian food <u>every evening/in the evening/for dinner</u>
- A visit/trip/went to the parliament building (in New Delhi)

NB: Every evening they had a party with Indian food would be awarded **2 marks**. They had a party with Indian food would get **0 marks** because there is no indication of regularity.

(e) • Two pupils showed her books which <u>they</u> (had) read <u>in German</u>

     NB: It must be clear that the pupils read the books

    • Three boys told her about <u>two weeks</u> they spent in <u>Hamburg/Germany</u> (with a church group) **OR** time spent in <u>Hamburg/Germany with a church group</u>

     NB: It must be clear that the three boys spent time in Germany

(f) **BOX 2:** She wants to promote understanding between the two countries

Text 3

(a) **BOX 2:** Sara's work is not perfect but she is a good pupil

(b) *Any three from:*

    • It was (great) <u>fun</u>

    • It is creative <u>work</u>

    • You can work with/use your hands

    • You can experiment with/try out <u>new ideas</u>

(c) • It <u>tasted</u> great/it was tasty/yummy/tasteful

    • They sold it/you could buy it in <u>the confectioner's/in the (cake) shop/bakery</u>

(d) • (Sitting/Passing/Doing well in) exams

    • <u>Developing/discovering/finding</u> new talent(s) (one verb needed)

     NB: Accept "new talents to discover/develop" despite awkward word order

(e) *Any two from:*

    • It offers (an) insight(s) into/a view/experience of (the world of) work/You see/saw into/become familiar with (the world of) work

    • You can <u>learn from/through</u> (your own) experience

    • You can <u>make/get/gain</u> (personal) contact(s)

Writing

Please see the assessment criteria for Writing on pages 102–104.

Listening

Item 1

(a) 13th August

(b) Four years ago

    OR

    When he was 11 years old

(c) *Any two from:*

    • (On) Wednesday(s)/every Wednesday

    • Every <u>second/other</u> weekend

    • <u>Four weeks</u> in the (school) holidays

(d) *Any two from:*

    • (Spends) Christmas/it with his mother

    • Visits/Sees/Stays with his dad <u>two days later</u>

    • He gets <u>two</u> lots of/<u>twice</u> as many presents/presents from <u>both</u> parents

(e) He (always) gets good marks/grades/results

(f) **BOX 3:** He is positive

Item 2

(a) (Martin is Erik's) <u>young(er)/little/small</u> brother

(b) *Any one from:*

    • They get on (quite) well

    OR

    • He has a good relationship with his brother/It is good

    • He <u>can</u> get on his nerves/he <u>sometimes/now and again</u> gets on his nerves/gets on his nerves when he comes into his room <u>without knocking</u>

    • He likes him

(c) • Mother: Secretary/Works in an office (in town)

     NB: Secretary in a bureau is acceptable

    • Father: Policeman/Police/Police officer

(d) His <u>mum</u> is allergic (to dogs)

    NB: Any recognisable spelling of "allergic" acceptable

(e) (i) Piano

    (ii) 3 years

(f) *Any three from:*

    • He has <u>three or four</u> (really) <u>good/close</u> friends

    • They are (quite) loud/noisy

    • Fun/funny/a good laugh

    • They have the same/similar interests

(g) *Any two from:*

    • Go jogging <u>in the (town) park</u>

    • Ride their bikes/go on <u>bike</u> rides/tours/cycle <u>in the (local)area/neighbourhood</u>

    • Play in/for the <u>school football team</u>/Play <u>football for the school</u>

    • Go to the cinema <u>regularly</u>

    • Watch <u>adventure</u> films

NATIONAL 5 GERMAN 2016

Reading

Text 1

(a) <u>Raw</u> material(s)/commodit<u>ies</u>

(b) • Put (a) <u>sticker(s)/sign(s)/message(s)</u>/note(s) saying <u>"No adverts"</u>

    OR

• Put (a) <u>sticker(s)/sign(s)/message(s)</u>/note(s) on the (house/front) <u>door</u>

(Candidate needs to mention either the message or where the message is to gain mark)

(c) • They come/are transported by <u>air/plane/are flown</u> in (to Germany) (ignore wrong tenses)

• This causes (air) pollution

(d) • It (often) <u>looks</u> <u>better</u>/<u>nicer</u> (insist on comparative)

• It is (usually) (much) cheap<u>er</u>/<u>more</u> reasonably priced/<u>better</u> value/<u>more</u> inexpensive/<u>less</u> expensive/not as expensive as a new one (insist on comparative)

(e) • (They can) exchange/swap <u>clothes</u>

• <u>Share</u> <u>sports</u> stuff/things/articles/gear/equipment

(f) (i) Try/attempt to <u>repair/fix</u> (broken) things/(a) bike(s)/(a) washing machine(s)

   (ii) Electrical equipment/goods/electronic<u>s</u>/appliance(s)

Text 2

(a) • <u>Hardly</u> any/not many/(a) few/<u>almost</u> no/<u>very</u> little

• **Tasteless/not tasty/doesn't taste nice/bad tasting (insist on suggestion of negative taste)**

(b) • The pupils/they do the cooking/cook/make their own food/lunch (themselves) (every day)

• Every 2 weeks another class is responsible for lunch

NB: A different class cooks every 2 weeks — 2 marks

NB: They cook for 2 weeks — 1 mark; lacks idea of rotation

(c) • The pupils no longer/don't heat up food/cook in the microwave/eat microwave food/use the microwave (when they go home)

• They (want to now) cook with/use <u>fresh</u> ingredients/they cook/eat <u>fresh</u> food/cook meals fresh

(d) • Accept/take (on) responsibility/be responsible

• Work <u>together</u>/<u>with others</u>/collaborate/cooperate/teamwork

• The cost of food/groceries/meals

(e) • The food is (now) tasty/tastier/delicious/yummy/nice(r)

• It/the food is now healthy/healthier/good for your health

• The pupils can get a <u>free</u> second helping/portion/two (meals) for the price of one   **(Any 2 from 3)**

Text 3

(a) • (You can) (always) do <u>what</u> you want/make your own decisions/choose what you want to do

• (You are) responsible for/in charge of (your own) <u>time</u> management/manage your (own) <u>time</u>

• (You can) <u>develop/spend time on/try out</u> your own ideas/make your <u>idea(s)</u> a reality   **(Any 2 from 3)**

(b) (i) (At the) <u>Sunday market/market in town</u>

(NB: market + one piece of information necessary to gain point)

   (ii) • <u>(Quite) a lot of/Many students</u> (have) bought his clothes/wear his clothes

• <u>He/I</u> began to see/saw his/my clothes/them <u>in/around/about town/in the street</u>

(c) • He had enough money for/bought/got/could afford a <u>used/second hand</u> car

• (Enough money for an) <u>eight-week</u> trip/journey/holiday through/to Italy

• He opened/got/had/started a (small) shop (in his home town)   **(Any 2 from 3)**

(d) • (You need) insurance

• (You need to) repair/fix (a) <u>sewing</u> machine(s)

                     (Any 1 from 2)

(e) They wanted to change/alter his jacket(s)/blazer(s) <u>and/or</u> shirt(s)

(f) **BOX 2:** It's worthwhile, although there are also difficulties
NB: no marks awarded for more than one tick

Writing

Please see the assessment criteria for Writing on pages 102–104.

Listening

Item 1

(a) • A <u>beach</u> house (on Corfu)

• A <u>holiday</u> flat/apartment (in Spain)

• A caravan (in the Alps)   **(Any 2 from 3)**

(b) • (You can) live/stay/spend time/be <u>together</u>

• (You can) <u>share</u> the work/<u>share</u> cooking/<u>share</u> washing up/(You can) <u>all</u> work/<u>all</u> cook/<u>all</u> wash up

• It's cheap<u>er</u> (than a hotel)

• (Maybe) your friends might speak another language   **(Any 1 from 4)**

(c) In (the) <u>south</u> (of) France (in a villa)

(d) In a (holiday) brochure/leaflet/pamphlet

(e) • Lying/relaxing/spending time <u>in the sun</u>/<u>sun</u>bathing

• Swimming <u>in the sea</u>

• Going to the (large) <u>shopping mall/centre(s)</u> (in the next town)   **(Any 2 from 3)**

(f) **BOX 2:** She's tried it and won't do it again

NB: no marks awarded for more than one tick

Item 2

(a) His boss/manager

(b) • Holidays <u>abroad</u> are not for her/she does not like holidays <u>abroad</u>

  • You can have a <u>good</u> holiday/time (in Germany)

  • You can go (everywhere) by car/Drive around

  • You can get to know the country/place/countryside/area/land (better) **(Any 2 from 4)**

(c) • (To forget) stress/a hectic life/It's stressful/hectic (in the town)

  • Peace/quiet is (very) important to him

  (Any 1 from 2)

(d) The <u>North Sea</u>/On the <u>north coast</u> (in a holiday home)

(e) The weather is/was bad/It rained (last year)(when he was there)/It rains (all the time)/wet

(f) • It's a compromise

  • It's not (too) far away

  • It's not (too) expensive/it's (very) cheap

  (Any 2 from 3)

(g) • She was/went/stayed/lived there (already) <u>with her sister</u>/<u>two years ago</u>

  NB: disregard "for two years"; it must be clear that event is in the past

  • She wants (to experience/see) something new

  (Any 1 from 2)

(h) • (It's good for) shopping/(Good) shopping facilities/opportunities/The shops

  • At home/At their (own) house/They are not going away

(j) Tidy/clean/clear out/sort out/organise the <u>garage</u>

Acknowledgements

Permission has been sought from all relevant copyright holders and Hodder Gibson is grateful for the use of the following:

Image © Rido/Fotolia (2014 Reading page 2);
Image © LifePhotoStudio/Shutterstock.com (2014 Reading page 4);
Image © Robin Heal/Shutterstock.com (2014 Reading page 6);
Image © wavebreakmedia/Shutterstock.com (2015 Reading page 2);
Image © OLJ Studio/Shutterstock.com (2015 Reading page 4);
Image © Pressmaster/Shutterstock.com (2015 Reading page 6);
Image © patpat/Shutterstock.com (2016 Reading page 2);
Image © Guy Shapira/Shutterstock.com (2016 Reading page 4);
Image © wavebreakmedia/Shutterstock.com (2016 Reading page 6).